Land Predators

Predators

John Stidworthy

Thomson Learning
New York

THE REMARKABLE WORLD

Dangerous Waters

MONSTERS OF THE DEEP
PIRATES AND TREASURE
VOYAGES OF EXPLORATION
THE WHALERS

Fearsome Creatures

BIRDS OF PREY
LAND PREDATORS
NIGHT CREATURES
WHEN DINOSAURS RULED THE EARTH

First published in the United States in 1996 by
Thomson Learning
New York, NY

Published simultaneously in Great Britain by Wayland
(Publishers) Ltd.

U.S. copyright © 1996 Thomson Learning

U.K. copyright © 1995 Wayland (Publishers) Ltd.

Library of Congress Cataloging-in-Publication Data
Stidworthy, John, 1943–
Land predators / John Stidworthy.
        p.   cm.—(Remarkable world)
    Includes bibliographical references (p.   ) and index.
    Summary: Examines such land predators as large meat-
eaters, killers that use poison, and animals that make traps.
    ISBN 1-56847-416-4
    1. Predatory animals—Juvenile literature. [1. Predatory
animals.] I. Title. II. Series.
QL758.S74   1996
591.53—dc20   95-25018

Printed in Italy

Picture acknowledgments

Bryan and Cherry Alexander 14t, 15b; Bruce Coleman Ltd. 6t/R.
I. M. Campbell, 7b/Gunter Ziesler, 9b/Norman Myers, 10t &
10b/Gunter Ziesler, 11b/Johnny Johnson, 18b/Austin James
Steven, 20t/George McCarthy, 22/Austin James Steven, 25b/Fritz
Prenzel, 27/John Cancalosi, 29b/C. B. & D. W. Frith, 30b/Gunter
Ziesler, 31m/Gunter Ziesler, 31b/A. J. Stevens, 32/Frieder Sauer,
34t/Jan Taylor, 39b/C. B. & D. W. Frith, 41m/Konrad Wothe,
42b/Frieder Sauer; Ecoscene *front cover, bottom left*, 20b; Frank
Lane Picture Agency 12b/W. Wisniewski, 16t/Frank W. Lane,
44t/R. Reynolds; NHPA *front cover, right*/Martin Wendler,
12m/Andy Rouse, 13/Gerard Lacz, 15t/Daniel Heuclin, 28/Karl
Switak, 30t/Martin Wendler, 33t/Daniel Heuclin, 34b/ANT,
41b/Stephen Dalton, 45b/ANT; Oxford Scientific Films *front cover,
middle left*/Anthony Bannister, 8/Tom McHugh/Photo Researchers
Inc., 15l/Konrad Wothe, 21t/Frank Schneidermeyer, 21b/Vivek R.
Sinha/Survival Anglia, 23t/Marty Cordano, 23b/Anthony Bannister,
25t/Breck P. Kent/Animals Animals, 29t/Ajay Desai, 33b/Tim
Shepherd, 35/Harry Fox, 36b/Liz & Tony Bomford/Survival
Anglia, 37/M. P. L. Fogden, 38/Robert Harvey/Survival Anglia,
39t/James H. Robinson, 45m/Densey Cline/Mantis Wildlife Films;
Papilio 18t, 36t, 40, 43; Zefa 1/Schafer, 5/Allstock/R. Lynn, 6b,
7t/Minden/F Lanting, 9t/Madison, 17/Allstock/Tom McHugh,
17/APL. The artwork is by Peter Bull 4, 11m, 14m; and Tony
Townsend 16b, 24, 26, 42m, 44b.

CONTENTS

MAN-EATING CATS

Although fewer in number today, lions still live in most parts of Africa south of the Sahara. They also used to live in western Asia and the north of India. Now only about three hundred Indian lions remain, living in the Gir Forest.

A large tented camp nestles in the African bush. As night closes in, lions begin to roar. The roars come closer and closer, until the sounds are nearly at the camp's edge. Suddenly they stop. In their tents, men sleep restlessly or lie awake, listening nervously. For an hour there is silence, then suddenly screams come from one tent. A lion has pushed its way in and seized a man from his bed. The lion drags its victim out and disappears into the darkness.

This scene was repeated dozens of times in 1898, during the construction of the railroad from the Kenya coast to the interior of Uganda. When the railroad reached the Tsavo River, thousands of workers gathered to build a bridge, and two lions began a reign of terror that lasted nine months. During this time, building was stopped for three weeks because of the danger from the lions. They killed and ate at least 28 Indian workers, and an even greater number of African workers, who had come to help build the railroad.

Right Only male lions have manes. They are black, as in this East African lion, or tawny, like the rest of the fur. The mane shows that the lion is male and also gives protection when two males fight. Although bigger and stronger than lionesses, males may let the females do most of the hunting, pushing in to claim dinner only after a kill is made.

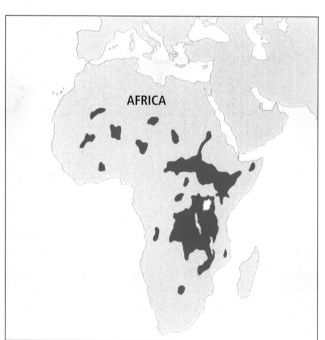

AFRICA

4

Most big cats are solitary animals, but lions live in groups called prides that can have four to six males and numerous females and cubs, totaling 25 or even more members. Prides are family groups, often led by an old lioness. Daughters stay with their pride, but young male lions leave.

Hunting the hunters

Traps were set, and hunters lay in wait for the man-eating Tsavo lions. The lions were cunning enough to avoid the traps. They hunted in unguarded parts of the camp. At first the hunters' efforts were in vain. Eventually Lieutenant Colonel Patterson, the engineer in charge of the railroad construction, rid the camp of the killers. After many nights, he shot one of the lions from a small 13-foot-high platform lashed to the top of four poles. He used a dead donkey as bait. This nearly proved fatal, as the lion ignored the carcass and spent two hours stalking around the platform before Patterson got a good enough view in the darkness to shoot the lion. A second lion, killed on a different night, was hit with six bullets before it finally died.

The lion that raided a railroad car

Far in the interior of Africa, in Uganda, other lions took to man-eating by the new railroad. They even attacked hunters who were lying in wait for them with guns. One night a German, an Italian, and an Englishman were keeping watch for lions from inside a railroad car. The German and Italian slept, while the Englishman, a man named Ryall, took his turn on watch. Suddenly pandemonium broke loose as a lion jumped through the window and seized Ryall by the throat. They crashed to the floor, pinning down the Italian and tipping the German from his bed. All the guns rolled out of reach. With Ryall in its mouth, the lion leaped out of the window.

When a lion bites, its long canine teeth stab into its prey. The incisor teeth between the canines nip and tear the skin. The teeth in the side of the mouth have sharp ridges and work like scissors to slice through the meat.

Three-legged killer

Some people say that lions become man-eaters when they are too old or feeble to kill their usual prey. In some cases, this may be true. In 1977, a lion in Tanzania killed eight people in three months. Hunters pursued it for weeks and eventually shot it. It was found to have only three legs.

However, many man-eaters look normal. There was nothing feeble about the Tsavo killers. They were large, strong lions that had simply found a new source of easy prey.

The lion's kill

Lions generally prey on animals such as zebra, wildebeest, impala, and other antelopes. They may also eat anything from insects to elephants and aren't above eating carrion. When they stalk prey they use any cover that is available to get close enough to make a sudden charge. A lion can weigh up to five hundred pounds and run a short distance at over 35 mph, so its sudden attack is devastating.

A lioness hidden in the dry grass watches intently as prey approaches. Only her eyes are lifted above the grass. She is so well hidden, and so still, that prey is unlikely to notice her until it is too late.

A lioness springs and slams into a wildebeest, sinking her canine teeth into its neck and spreading her claws to spike and hold its body. Lions do not hunt every day. A large meal is often followed by a long rest. A lion may spend most of the day asleep and feed only once or twice a week.

A lion tries to knock down its prey quickly, breaking the animal's neck with its paws and teeth or swiftly suffocating the animal. Sometimes the first attack fails, or the intended meal turns the tables. A buffalo can gore a lion with its horns. A giraffe can kill a lion with a kick. Even porcupines have killed lions by backing their quills into the lions' paws and faces, leaving wounds that get infected and slowly kill the king of beasts.

Although some tigers live in tropical jungles, they also live in Siberia, where they have to contend with snow in the winter. They have thick fur coats to help.

Largest cats

The tiger of Asia is usually about the same size as a lion, but the tigers that live in Siberia and Manchuria are the biggest of all cats. Some males weigh more than five hundred pounds, are higher than three feet at the shoulder, and measure ten feet from nose to tail. As with other cats, females are smaller than males.

In India, tigers generally hunt sambar deer and wild boar but, like lions, they will eat anything from a frog to a young elephant, given the chance. Unlike the lion, the tiger is usually a solitary hunter. It may drag its prey to a quiet place to feed. It can pull a large deer for up to half a mile and is strong enough to haul away a cow.

A leopard drags away an antelope bigger than itself. A solitary hunter, often lying in wait up a tree or in heavy cover, the leopard may be difficult to see.

Leopard at the picnic

The leopard lives in Africa and Asia. It is at home in the forest and is a good climber. It catches all kinds of prey, from monkeys to antelope. Like the lion and tiger, it sometimes turns to hunting people, but it seems to have a particular taste for dogs.

In 1885 a group of Europeans were enjoying a grand picnic at the bottom of a cliff in northwest India. In addition to the 40 guests, there was a small army of cooks and servants working away behind some nearby boulders. The host's dogs, two white terriers, ran around among the guests.

One guest, Major Alexander, glanced up to the sky and saw a leopard's head. It peered over the cliff, 50 yards above the group. He remarked to his neighbor that the leopard was after the terriers. "Nonsense," said his friend. "No leopard would come near such a large gathering of people."

Major Alexander suggested tying up the dogs, but nobody listened. Ten minutes later, the leopard crept down the cliff. It rushed through the picnicking crowd, seized a terrier, and carried it off in its jaws before anyone could react.

The best climber of the big cats, the leopard often carries its meal up a tree, away from other predators. It may come back to this "larder" for a second feast.

Even though tigers are getting rare, they are unpopular in many parts of India because they catch domestic animals and can be a danger to humans. Most are shy, but a few turn to man-eating. One that was shot in 1911 is reputed to have killed 438 people in eight years.

Left An Indian tiger plunges into the water in pursuit of a sambar deer. Many cats avoid water, but tigers don't mind swimming and will go into water to cool off.

Facing your attacker

The Sundarbans region near Calcutta in India consists of the vast, swampy delta of the Ganges River. There are many low-lying islands covered in reeds and jungle. Tigers live there and swim from island to island in search of prey. Forestry workers are sometimes attacked by tigers hiding in the dense vegetation. Tigers usually pounce from behind on unsuspecting prey. Someone realized that tigers never attacked people who were facing them. The workers are now given masks with faces painted on them to wear on the backs of their heads, and the number of tiger attacks has dropped.

The menacing snarl of a big male tiger is an unwelcome sound to forest workers. As well as face masks, dummies that look like humans but give an electric shock have helped deter tigers from attacking people.

THE BIGGEST MEAT-EATERS

Brown bears live across North America, Europe, and northern Asia, varying little in size and color from place to place. In parts of North America and Europe where humans are common, bears are now rare.

The biggest of all the Carnivora, the meat-eating mammals, are the brown bears that live in parts of Alaska, particularly on and around Kodiak Island. Captive specimens have been measured at ten feet from nose to stubby tail, and more than 1,600 pounds in weight. If it stands on its hind legs, a bear that size is twice as tall as a grown man. Even an average Kodiak bear is about eight feet long and weighs 1,100 pounds. Brown bears vary in weight through the year. They are heaviest in the autumn when they have fed well and are thinnest in the spring after starving during their hibernation.

A grizzly bear savors a juicy salmon. A grizzly is a variety of brown bear that lives in North America. These large animals eat all types of food and make use of all kinds of terrain. They can swim and even climb if necessary.

Right A Kodiak brown bear raises itself on its hind legs to sniff the wind or peer at something it does not recognize.

Below A brown bear scoops out salmon in quick succession.

Although technically carnivores, and capable of killing animals as big as elk, brown bears feed mainly on berries, roots, and tender leaves. They will also eat insect grubs, mice, fish, deer, and dead animals. Brown bears are aggressive animals, especially when they have cubs. They rely on their sense of smell more than their vision, which is rather poor. Some scientists think that many attacks on humans are made because they are mistaken for rival bears. By the time the bears realize their mistake it is too late. They rarely eat human victims and seem to dislike the smell of people.

Salmon fishing

When salmon swim from the sea up rivers to spawn, North American brown bears have one of their best feeding seasons. Bears gather from far and wide in large groups, quite unlike their usual solitary, aggressive behavior. Each waits beside or in a pool and hooks fish as the salmon struggle to leap up the rapids against the strong current.

Arctic adaptations

Polar bears are almost as big as Kodiak bears. They evolved from brown bears only a few thousand years ago, as they became adapted to life in Arctic conditions. They have tiny earflaps and six-inch-thick fur to cut down on heat loss. Polar bears can roam around in temperatures as low as -40°F. The only bare skin is the black nose-tip and the pads on the feet; even the soles of the feet have fur to help the bear keep its grip on the ice.

Much of the "land" that polar bears hunt on is actually ice. At some times of year, the ice may melt or break up and drift, so polar bears need to be able to swim well. One was seen at sea more than 180 miles from the nearest coast.

A polar bear swims in a version of the dog paddle. It is very agile in the water, although the seals it preys upon can swim much faster and are able to escape easily from a swimming bear.

Living on a high-fat diet

As few plants grow in the high Arctic, polar bears are mainly meat-eaters. Up to 90 percent of the average polar bear's diet consists of seals. Bears wait next to seals' breathing holes for long periods until one surfaces and can be swatted with a paw and pulled from the water. One blow of a polar bear's paw can smash a seal's skull. The bear eats the whole seal and especially likes the thick layer of blubber, or fat, under the seal's skin. Bears also stalk seals and other animals across the ice and snow. The Inuit say that when the polar bear is stalking it covers its black nose with a paw for better camouflage.

Left A polar bear waits until a seal cruising below the ice comes within range at the breathing hole.

Below Polar bears live mainly on the ice of the Arctic.

The bear's revenge

Travelers in the Arctic can also be a target for polar bears. Several explorers have complained of a polar bear appearing on the horizon and heading straight toward them, with no change of pace or expression until it launched an attack. Over the years, many people have been killed by polar bears. But more bears have been killed by people, either for their fur or to eat, although today they are protected by law. Some bears that have been eaten have had their revenge after their deaths. Hungry Arctic explorers have died from eating polar bear liver, which contains large amounts of Vitamin A. This vitamin is good for humans in small amounts, but too much can be fatal.

As dangerous as the average bear

Bears of all kinds are powerful enough to kill humans. This is regularly proved in American national parks, where the relatively small black bears are used to visitors in cars. They look friendly and tame. Each year a small number of people get out of their cars for a better look—and never return.

Right A young black bear in a safari park investigates an automobile. The humans would be as foolish to get out here as they would be if they saw a bear in the wild.

Garbage dumps bring danger

At the town of Churchill, on the western shore of Canada's Hudson Bay, polar bears regularly clash with people. The bears visit the area in spring and autumn, using the town's garbage dump as a source of food. Some bears wander into town. It is not safe to be out after dark, and armed people have to patrol during the day. In 1983 a bear killed a man on the town's main street. Now the bears are often tranquilized, captured, and flown many miles into the wilderness. Unfortunately, polar bears are used to traveling long distances, and some of them soon find their way back. But the polar bears are not all bad news for Churchill: in some years they have brought two million dollars to the town, from visitors flocking to see them.

A tranquilized polar bear **(above)** is scooped up in a net under a helicopter so that it can be carried back to the wilderness. There are still many more **(right)** wanting to sample a garbage dump.

POISONOUS KILLERS

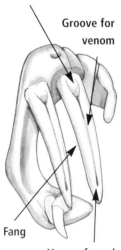

Cobras and some other venomous snakes have rigid fangs with a duct running from top to tip to carry venom.

Venom duct

Groove for venom

Fang

Venom forced out of this opening

Location of fangs

IN 1957, a small snake arrived at a museum to be identified by the museum's snake expert. As it was being inspected, it bit the expert. Twenty-four hours later the man was dead. The man this happened to was Dr. Karl Schmidt, one of the most famous reptile experts of the twentieth century. A true scientist to the last, he kept an hourly record of his symptoms, which included sickness and bleeding from the mouth, before his breathing stopped and he died. He had massive internal bleeding in several parts of his body.

Dr. Schmidt had been bitten by a boomslang, one of the grass snake family. Most grass snakes are harmless, but some have venom glands that release poison down small, grooved fangs at the back of the mouth. These snakes need to get a good grip to inject any poison, and most have weak venom, suitable only for overcoming small prey. They were once all believed to be harmless to humans.

The boomslang has an inefficient means of injecting poison, but its venom is stronger than that of many vipers. It is a tree snake and usually catches lizards. It rarely bites people, but it is lethal if it does. The bird-eating snake, another African rear-fanged snake, has also killed humans.

A male boomslang looks down from a branch. More than six feet long, this snake has large eyes and good eyesight. The eyes partly face forward. This probably helps it judge distances as it climbs and also when it strikes at prey. Its scales have backward-facing keels, which help grip bark as the snake climbs.

Fangs and venom

Most venomous snakes have fangs at the front of the mouth. The fangs can be short and rigid—as in the case of cobras—or long and hinged—as in vipers and rattlesnakes.

Looking straight into a diamondback rattlesnake's mouth

A black mamba is held ready for milking. Venom is squeezed from the venom glands and is collected as it runs from the fangs. The venom can be used to produce an antidote.

In general, cobras produce nerve poisons that paralyze and produce heart failure in their victims, whereas vipers produce venom that affects body tissues, causing bleeding or clotting of the blood. Actually, most venomous snakes inject a cocktail of several poisonous substances in their victims, producing both types of effect in varying degrees. The venom is powerful, and not much is needed to have an effect. A very large rattlesnake holds about a tenth of an ounce of liquid venom.

Snakebite fatalities

There are antidotes to many types of snake venom, but for these to work they need to be given soon after the bite, and the snake must be identified correctly. In many parts of the world where there are poisonous snakes, medical attention may not be quickly available, and snakebite is still a significant death risk.

Lethal doses

The strength of venom is often estimated after it has been dried, so it seems like a smaller amount. A large cobra can contain 600 mg (two-one hundredths of an ounce) of venom. The lethal dose for a human is usually less than 20 mg, so such a cobra holds enough to kill 30 people. A lethal dose from a boomslang is only about 5 mg of venom.

On this fingertip is a crystal of cobra venom. Dissolved again, it would be lethal if injected. It contains enough poison to kill six people.

Deadly Australian snakes

In Australia, the one part of the world where there are more venomous snakes than harmless ones, there are relatively few deaths from snakes. The Australian fierce snake has the most powerful venom among land snakes. The ten-foot long taipan and the tiger snake also have

The Australian taipan has a reputation for being aggressive—and deadly.

very powerful venom, but most of them live away from human habitation and avoid people if possible.

It has been estimated that more than 40,000 deaths from snakebite occur in the world each year. Of these, about 1,000 are in Africa, 2,000 or so in Brazil, and up to 15,000 in India, mainly from Russell's vipers and cobras. The statistics are not completely reliable, but suggest that the worst risk is in tropical countries where many people go barefoot.

Poisonous giants

Most venomous snakes feed on small animals such as rats, mice, lizards, and birds, which they stun quickly with their venom. A surprising number of snakes feed on other snakes. This is true

of the hamadryad, or king cobra, the largest of all venomous snakes. This cobra grows to 18 feet long and eats other snakes of all kinds, including pythons and other cobras. It has a large venom gland, and its poison can kill an elephant in four hours.

The only venomous snake in northern Europe is the adder. It is rarely seen except when basking in the sun. It only bites when provoked.

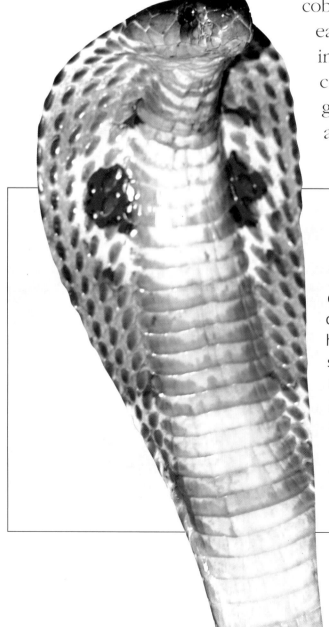

Avoiding trouble

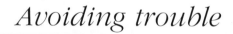

The classic pose of the Indian cobra, with its hood spread by special ribs in the neck region, is a response to a threat. Most of the time the neck is narrow.

Most snakes are shy animals, and even those with powerful weapons often avoid conflict if they can.

The false eyes on the hood of a cobra and the rattle on the end of a rattlesnake's tail are ways of chasing off a potential enemy. The snakes' venom is therefore not used for defense, but can be saved for catching meals.

This Gaboon viper has stabbed a mouse. As well as injecting venom, the huge fangs can help rake the prey into the mouth.

This 12-foot-long king cobra has killed an 8-foot-long rat snake and is getting ready to swallow it whole.

The fangs of the huge hamadryad are only half an inch long. These are dwarfed by the hinged fangs of many of the vipers. The biggest fangs are those of the Gaboon viper of Africa, which are up to two inches long. When the viper opens its mouth wide, the fangs swing out, ready to be plunged into the victim. Viper venom is slower-acting than the venom of cobras, but it is still deadly to the prey. Often the viper just stabs its victim, injects venom, and then lets go. The victim may wander off a short distance to die, but the viper tracks it down.

Not a nice type

A "type specimen" is the very first animal of its species to be given a scientific name and description. That individual is usually kept in a museum so scientists can check their specimens against it to see if they are the same. The type specimen of the Javanese krait—a snake of the cobra family—is a little unusual. Before its capture, this snake killed the father and son of a family asleep in their hut in Java.

Lizards and arachnids

Of the 2,600 species of snake, nearly one-third are venomous, but far fewer are dangerous to humans. Most are found in tropical regions, where all types of reptiles are most common. In contrast, only two species of lizards out of about 3,700 are venomous.

The ringhals is a cobra from southern Africa. Pretending to be dead is one of its ways of deterring enemies. It can also spray venom from its fangs toward the eyes of an attacker. As a last resort, it bites.

These are the Gila monster and the beaded lizard, found in the southwestern United States and Mexico. The lizard's venom glands are in the lower jaw, and it has to chew on its victims to inject the poison. The venom is effective on small mammals, lizards, and other creatures. These lizards can give a painful bite to a human, which can lead to numbness and some paralysis, but they rarely kill healthy humans. There are many stories in the old West of fatal lizard bites, but in many cases poor health—or too much whiskey—were more fatal than the lizard.

Scorpions are arachnids that usually prey on insects and spiders. Some catch small lizards and mammals. The large claws are their main weapon and are usually strong enough to kill and tear the food. Scorpions use their sting if the prey struggles, but it

A Gila monster feeds on a kangaroo rat. Gila monsters grow to about 20 inches long and spend much of their time underground.

A sting in the tail

In the United States there are far more deaths from scorpion stings than from snake bites. In Arizona, between 1929 and 1948, scorpions killed twice as many people as all other kinds of venomous animals combined. Many scorpions hide under stones, but the insides of shoes or beds can be a good substitute. If the unfortunate owner steps or lies on them, the scorpions sting.

An African desert scorpion has seized a locust, and its poison sting is raised, ready to strike.

is mainly used in defense. The scorpion brings its tail over its head, and the poison-filled bulb on the end pumps venom down the sting as it stabs into the enemy. The stings of most of the six hundred kinds of scorpion are not much worse than wasp stings. The tropical forest scorpions—the largest of all—have relatively weak stings and rarely use them. A few of the small desert scorpions of the United States and the Middle East have the deadliest stings, with effects like cobra bites. In 1957 1,494 people died in Mexico from scorpion stings. People living in scorpion country are wise to check their shoes before putting them on.

Venomous spiders

All spiders have venom. They use fangs to inject paralyzing doses into their prey. Insects are their usual prey, but some large tropical spiders may catch small mice, lizards, frogs, or even baby birds. Bird-eating spiders, in spite of their large size and fangs, are placid and not really dangerous to humans. Those that are aggressive can give a painful bite, but deaths are rare.

Of the more than 30,000 known kinds of spiders in the world, one in a thousand may be dangerous to people. The Brazilian wandering spider is probably the most dangerous. It often lurks in clothes and shoes, and just 0.1 mg of its venom is enough to kill a human. The venom causes pain, muscular spasms, and sweating and can kill in just a few hours. Luckily an antidote is now available.

This is an enlarged view of a spider's chelicera—one of a pair in front of the mouth. It forms a "hypodermic syringe" to inject venom from the poison glands at its base. The pointed, movable tip is called the fang.

Venom duct

Venom gland

Fang

Location of fangs

Black widows and funnel-webs

A black widow spider in her web awaits prey. Her legs are touching strands whose movement will signal the approach of prey.

The best-known poisonous spider is the black widow. Found in many of the warmer parts of the world, it has a variety of names, such as the shoe-button and, in Australia, the redback. Its venom contains substances that quickly paralyze insect prey and destroy the prey's nervous system. These substances also damage nerves in mammals and are the reason for the painfulness of the black widow's bite.

Apart from pain, the bite produces other symptoms in humans, including paralysis, sickness, dizziness, and great anxiety. The venom is over ten times more powerful than some rattlesnake venom, but it is rarely fatal. Out of about 1,300 reported bites over nearly 200 years in the United States, only 55 people have died. These victims were mostly young or sick. There is now an antidote available that lessens the risk of death, if not the pain. The black widow likes secluded hiding places. Unfortunately, some choose to live under the seats of outdoor toilets in rural areas and can bite people in very tender places.

The Sydney funnel-web spider of Australia is much more dangerous. It produces many uncomfortable symptoms, and death from heart and breathing failure can follow less than 12 hours after a bite.

The aggressive look of a funnel-web spider getting ready to strike is no bluff. The sharp fangs can be seen beneath the head.

SWALLOWING PREY WHOLE

Apart from the braincase, the bones in a snake's skull are less firmly attached to one another than are those in a human. Snakes grow new teeth throughout their lives, replacing old and worn ones.

MANY lizards and birds seize small prey, which they then swallow almost whole. But the champion swallowers are the big constricting snakes, the pythons and boas. All snakes swallow their food whole. They have no means of breaking it into pieces because their teeth are sharp and point backward, for biting rather than grinding. Snakes can swallow surprisingly big animals in relation to their own width; sometimes the prey is much wider than its captor.

Elastic jaws

Snakes have extremely flexible jaws that are attached to the skull by elastic ligaments. The upper jaws can swing up and out to increase the size of the mouth. The attachments for the lower jaw can swing outward and downward to open the jaw wide. The two halves of the bottom jaw are attached to one another at the front by a single elastic ligament, which also allows the mouth to stretch. The snake eases its mouth around the prey, then eases the separate jaw bones forward one by one, the sharp teeth taking a grip.

A carpet python shows the enormous gape of its jaws as it gradually swallows a bird it has caught. The bird's head is already in the snake's throat, but it will take a while for the bird to be totally swallowed and to travel down to the snake's stomach, which is about one-third of the way down the snake. This python grows to ten feet or more, but can climb well, gripping tree branches with its tail.

The egg-eater

One of the most spectacular swallowers is the African egg-eating snake. It grows to about 30 inches long, but is quite skinny. It usually moves through trees, detecting the nests of small birds and eating their eggs, but a full-grown snake can swallow a hen's egg whole. The egg is cracked open in the snake's gullet and the snake digests the contents but spits out the fragments of shell.

As this snake swallows a hen's egg, its skin is pulled so that the scales and the skin between them are stretched paper-thin.

Slowly the mouth engulfs the food, and then waves of muscular contraction carry it down the throat into the stomach. Snakes are always careful to start at the head of prey. That way, the prey's legs fold backward as the snake swallows.

Feasting

Because of their size, large pythons can deal with enormous meals. The reticulated python of Southeast Asia often grows to over 20 feet long—the longest ever recorded was 30 feet. However, it is a relatively slim snake and tends to feed on rats and other small animals, although sometimes it may kill and swallow wild pigs. The Asiatic rock python does not grow as long, but it is a bulkier animal and regularly kills small deer. One is even known to have killed and eaten a leopard.

young
eticulated
ython kills an
dult rat by
onstriction.
he victim looks
oo big for the
nake, but
nakes rarely
nisjudge their
rey. Swallowed
ead first, the
egs pinned to
ne body, the rat
vill eventually
e swallowed.

Swallowing a meal this size can take several hours. The food also takes a long time to digest, and the lump in the snake's stomach may be visible for days afterward. Such a huge meal provides plenty of nourishment, and it may be weeks before the snake needs to eat again.

Fasting

Some snakes are capable of going without food for a year or more. Because they eat infrequently, the feeding habits of snakes in zoos are well documented.

Above
An Asiatic rock python swallows a chital deer. These deer stand almost three feet tall at the shoulder and weigh 60 pounds or more.

Pythons in the London Zoo in England have gone for more than a year without eating. A reticulated python in the Frankfurt Zoo in Germany fasted for 22 months. These snakes were still healthy after their fasts.

An anaconda holds a caiman in its powerful coils as it waits for the caiman to die.

The boa constrictor of South America grows to 10 or 12 feet long. Rodents are its usual diet, but a boa can catch small cats, such as ocelots. The water-loving anaconda grows much larger. There are many arguments about its maximum size, but it may reach, or even exceed, the 30-foot length of the biggest pythons. The anaconda is a very bulky snake. One specimen was 19 feet long, weighed 235 pounds, and measured 3 feet around the thickest part of its body. Anacondas feed on caimans (relatives of alligators), tapirs, and piglike peccaries.

The largest meal in history?

The biggest snake meal ever measured was an impala weighing 130 pounds, which was swallowed by an African rock python 16 feet long, in 1950.

The Thomson's gazelle disappearing into this African rock python is about half the size of an impala. The python surprised this fast-running animal.

All these slide easily down the snake's gullet. They also eat rodents, which can be as big as the capybara—the world's largest rodent—at 4 feet long and 145 pounds.

Killer coils

All pythons and boas catch their prey by constriction. They throw their coils around a victim and then use their enormous muscle power to squeeze its chest and stop its breathing. The prey is suffocated rather than crushed. These snakes are very powerful—any constrictor larger than about 13 feet is probably strong enough to kill a person. However, there are few recorded human deaths from these giant snakes. Pythons are more likely to be caught and eaten by humans than the other way around. It is doubtful whether even the biggest pythons could get their jaws around the shoulders of an adult human in order to swallow it, but children may be at risk. In 1927, a 17-foot-long reticulated python swallowed a 14-year-old boy living in the Talaud Islands of Indonesia. In 1960 an eight-year-old boy went to his family's paddy field at Cox's Bazaar, Bangladesh, to gather some rice. He was attacked and suffocated by a python 20 feet long.

Thomson's gazelle has long horns that make it hard to swallow. Here the python uses its squeezing pressure to break the horns, making a more comfortable meal.

Workers in an African snake park handle rock pythons. Snakes this size, unless tame, may be too much for one person to handle.

THE SMALLEST PREDATORS

A white-toothed shrew shown from below displays the sharp teeth that give it its name and the long whiskers around the snout that help it feel its way.

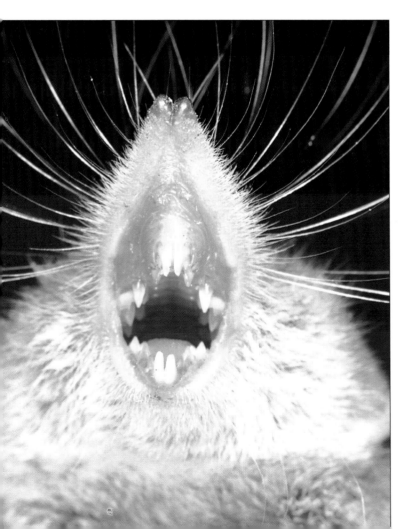

SHREWS are among the smallest of all mammals, yet they are also among the fiercest. In its short life—about one to four years—a shrew kills many more animals than a lion does during its 15- to 25-year lifetime. Many of the shrew's victims are quite small, ranging from insects to earthworms, but some kinds of shrews catch mice or birds. The common shrew, which is found across most of Europe, has a body less than 3 inches long with a tail of about 1.5 inches, and it weighs no more than half an ounce. Its favorite foods are insect larvae, beetles, wood lice, and earthworms. Sometimes it attacks worms that are twice as long as itself. It also eats spiders, centipedes, slugs, and snails. It can run to chase its prey, or it may dig stationary prey, such as insect pupae, from the soil.

A white-toothed shrew finishes off an insect before rushing on to the next meal. This shrew lives in continental Europe and North Africa. It moves through the leaf litter, feeling for insects and other small animals with its sensitive snout.

Ever-hungry hunters

Compared to its small size, a shrew's body has a large surface area through which it can lose heat very quickly. It therefore uses a lot of energy in keeping warm, and it must replace this energy constantly. As it runs around searching for food, it uses even more energy. Not surprisingly, a common shrew eats nearly its own weight in food every day.

Pygmy shrews are even smaller, with a body between 1.5 and 2.5 inches long and a tail about three-quarters of its body length. Their maximum weight is about a fifth of an ounce. These little predators, with their razor-sharp teeth, capture hundreds of small creatures because they have to eat one and a quarter times their own weight in food every day. The Etruscan shrew, found in southern Europe and in parts of Africa and Asia, is about as small as a mammal can be. It weighs a maximum of .07 ounces, but has to eat a much greater weight of food daily.

Below This pygmy shrew probably weighs much less than the earthworm it is attacking. Pygmy shrews move very fast, as though they are in a speeded-up film. Their high-pitched twittering can often be heard as they hunt through tunnels in low-growing vegetation.

Quick starvation

It is not surprising that shrews are active most of the time, day and night. If they go much more than two hours without food, they may starve to death. They run through the vegetation on the ground, sometimes in tunnels beneath a layer of dead leaves, and sometimes underground. Shrews have nests to which they may return for short periods of rest.

Killer "mice"

Shrews of various kinds live over most of the world, but not in Australia. Here marsupial "mice" and "rats" take their place. The planigale is the smallest marsupial, at not much more than two inches long, but it is a ferocious beast that hunts at night, killing grasshoppers nearly as large as itself. Other marsupial mice, such as the dunnart, kill vertebrates as well as insects. The mulgara kills ordinary mice by springing on them and biting their necks.

Above A dunnart feasts on a large grasshopper.

It then neatly turns back the victim's skin from head to tail, as it munches its way down the rest of the mouse.

Below This mulgara has caught a mouse. The mulgara is about six inches long, not counting its tail. This one was photographed near Ayers Rock in central Australia. These tough little animals can withstand extremes of heat and cold in the desert.

They sometimes take short naps in the middle of hunting—tucking their noses into their chests and staying completely motionless for a few seconds and then waking up to continue their search for food.

A shrew must stay active even in the winter. It is too small to store fat and hibernate, so it has to keep hunting, although it spends as much time as possible below the surface rather than in the cold air.

Assassins at large

Even among tiny animals, such as insects, there are many ferocious killers. The members of one large group of insects known as "bugs" have mouth parts built for piercing and sucking. Most bugs, such as aphids, shieldbugs, scale insects, and whiteflies, are plant feeders that use their mouth parts to suck plant juices. Some bugs, though, have different diets. The assassin bugs have piercing mouth parts that they use to stab other animals, often holding them with their strong, bristly legs. They inject digestive juices that paralyze their prey and dissolve their insides so they can be easily sucked up. Most assassin bugs feed on insects, but some can give painful bites to people.

A large assassin bug ensures its survival in a North American desert by capturing a grasshopper.

Death in the garden

Another killer that can be found in many gardens is the ladybug. Both the adults and the larvae have powerful jaws, and occasionally they nip people. They feed on other insects, such as aphids—like the aphids that live on roses—chewing up vast numbers of them. The larvae eat constantly, as they climb to the top of a rose and then work their way down, exploring all the side shoots for prey.

A two-spotted ladybug tackles a plant stem full of blackflies. The ever-hungry ladybug is very helpful to gardeners, foresters, and farmers.

Killers on the march

Almost nothing compares with army ants in their ability to kill and eat everything in their path. The army ants of South America are nomadic, staying in one spot for just a few weeks while they tend their eggs and young. When the eggs hatch and new worker ants emerge from the pupae, the time has come to move on. The ants kill so many of the creatures nearby that they would run out of food if they stayed too long.

When they hunt, the ants stream from the nest in a column. The large soldier ants, with their big jaws, defend the sides of the column. Even the smaller workers have very powerful jaws.

Below Soldier ants raid a termites' nest in Malawi, Africa, and carry off their victims to eat.

When the column finds food, it swarms all over it, biting, stinging, and cutting it to pieces. Any animal that cannot fly away is in danger. The ants attack grubs, caterpillars, beetles, and other insects. They ransack the nests of wasps, bees, and termites, carrying away the young and eating them. They eat mice and rats and devour any large animals that are tied up or too slow to escape. They eat the food on the spot or carry it away and bury it on the route of the march.

A column of army ants in the Central American rain forest has found a wasps' nest. A big wasp grub is being carried off by a group of worker ants.

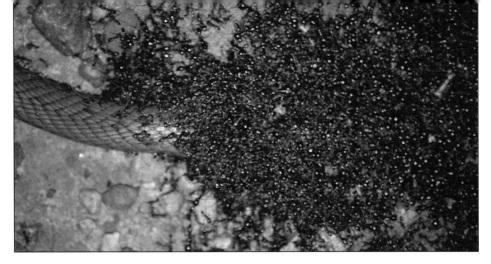

African driver ants mass on the remains of a cobra. It is being torn to pieces by thousands of tiny jaws.

Returning to base

When the ants have been on the move for a few hours, they retrace their steps, picking up their buried food stores and taking them back to the "bivouac," the temporary camp where they have left the colony's queen and some guard ants. In some tropical American species, the bivouac is simply a sheltered spot, perhaps under a log, where the workers cluster into a huge protective ball three feet across, with the queen and the young in the middle. A colony may contain as many as 700,000 ants.

Millions of mouths

Some African species, called driver ants, live in even bigger colonies that may contain up to 20 million ants. Their marching feet can be heard by humans as a column passes. Their bivouacs are nests with underground tunnels, and last longer than those of South American army ants. Raiding parties go out in columns that are almost unstoppable. Driver ants have extremely powerful jaws. They sometimes catch pythons that are too full from their last meal to flee; the snakes are reduced to skeletons within a few hours.

Praying for dinner?

The praying mantis is a small but efficient killer. Instead of chasing prey, the mantis waits in one spot, relying on its camouflage to make it invisible. It folds its front legs up near its face, looking as though it is praying, while its big eyes remain watchful. When a suitable insect approaches, the mantis waits until the victim is within range. Then its front legs straighten, grasp the food, and fold again in a flash. Spines on the legs hold the prey in place while the mantis bites into it, and the powerful jaws munch up the whole animal, even if it is a hard-skinned insect.

The large eyes of a mantis face forward, above strong chewing jaws.

While stalking prey, a small gecko lizard meets its own end in the grasp of a praying mantis in a Thailand forest.

Death in disguise

Apart from the praying mantis of Europe, there are about 1,800 other species found in the warm parts of the world. Some tropical species can tackle lizards and birds. Most have colors that blend with their surroundings, and many have shapes that mimic twigs or leaves. Some of the most spectacular are the flower mantises, which mimic the shape and color of the flowers in which they lurk. They prey on insects attracted to the flowers' nectar.

Is this a beautiful flower? An orchid perhaps? No—it is a deadly flower mantis sitting on a leaf, waiting for its next meal.

Grasshoppers, butterflies, and flies are the mantis's usual diet, but sometimes mantises are cannibals. A female may even attack and eat the smaller male while he is mating with her.

Reptilian sharpshooters

Many species of lizards wait in ambush until prey comes close enough to be caught with a sudden rush and grab. Chameleons go one better by snatching prey with their long, sticky tongues.

Chameleons have narrow bodies and feet that grasp branches well. They are colored to blend with their surroundings in trees or bushes, and some can even change their colors. They move slowly and carefully, one leg at a time. Everything about them seems designed to avoid being seen, so that potential prey does not know they are there.

A fly is picked off a leaf by the deadly accurate shooting of a Mediterranean chameleon's tongue. The thick tip of the tongue is wrapped around the prey, and both the chameleon's eyes are watching the spot where the fly was standing.

The chameleon's eyes are on little turrets at the side of its head. Each eye moves separately to scan the surroundings, but they can both be focused on food in front of its head. A chameleon can line up its head accurately and judge exactly when prey is within range of its tongue. Its tongue can extend to the length of its body and tail combined, so the prey may be some distance from the chameleon when the tongue muscles squeeze and the tongue tip shoots forward. The flick of the tongue is almost too fast for a human eye to see. The tip is sticky, and it also has a grasping action. Once the chameleon takes aim, its prey is nearly always doomed.

A close-up of a chameleon's eye

TRAPPED!

THE ant lion is a predatory insect related to lacewings. Most kinds of ant lions live in the tropics. The adults look and behave somewhat like dragonflies and hunt other insects in flight. The larvae of the ant lion have a less energetic, but very effective, way of trapping their dinners.

Below An ant slides to its death in the ant lion larva's trap.

The pitfall

The ant lion larva digs a pit in sandy soil. Then it buries itself at the bottom, concealing its soft body but leaving its vicious jaws above the surface. If an ant steps on the edge of the pit, it slips down the loose sand grains and falls into the vise-like jaws of the ant lion.

Below The serrated jaws of the ant lion hold an ant and inject digestive juices. They then suck out the resulting "soup."

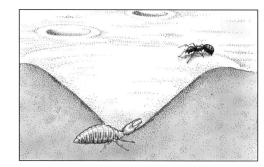

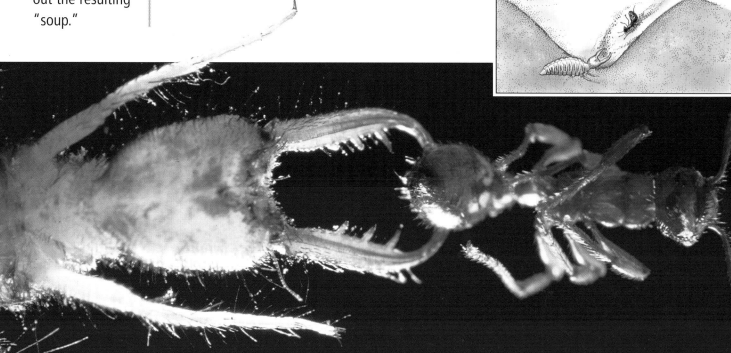

In Europe, the tiger beetle larva also burrows in sandy soil and lies in wait. The burrow is just wide enough for the larva, and the head and neck plug the opening. The larva waits to snatch an unsuspecting insect walking on the surface.

Spider silk

The best examples of trap-makers among land animals are spiders. They can produce silk from special structures—called spinnerets—on their abdomens. Inside the spinnerets are silk glands. The silk is liquid when it is produced, but hardens into thread when it hits the air.

Some spiders produce traps that are a sheet of crisscrossed fibers. The large house spider makes this type of web. It lives in one rolled-up corner. When an insect lands on the web, its feet get caught in the maze of fibers. The spider feels it struggling and rushes out for the kill.

The spider uses spinnerets on its abdomen to spin its web. Spiders don't have to learn how to spin their complex webs; it is something they do automatically.

Hammock webs

Small round "money spiders" make slightly more complex webs than house spiders. They make a flat sheet of fibers in which they lie in wait, but they also stretch vertical fibers to the vegetation above and below the web. On autumn mornings, you may see hundreds of these little webs, shining *with dew, covering the bushes. Flying insects snag themselves in the vertical lines and fall down. When they hit the flat sheet, the money spider gives a fatal bite.*

This gorse bush is covered with dozens of hammock webs—the work of money spiders.

Orb webs

The webs of orb web spiders are beautiful, but deadly. They usually hang vertically, and some of the threads are sticky, making escape difficult for any insect that blunders in. The spider constructs the web in a precise way, to create a masterpiece of engineering. It makes an outline frame, and then radial lines (from the center to the sides), followed by spirals of silk. An average web may have more than 1,000 points where silk threads join and 65 feet of thread in total. The web is very light, but extremely strong. Even so, it gets wear and tear, so many orb web spiders make new webs each day. They eat the old web, so there is little waste. Orb web spiders often live away from the web but they stay in touch by running a signal thread from the web to their hiding places. In this way, they can feel the vibrations caused by prey struggling in the web.

Stages in the construction of a typical orb web

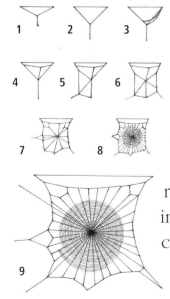

Tough web

The Nephila spider of Southeast Asia makes webs up to seven feet in diameter. These are strong enough to slow down a human, and the spiders sometimes catch and eat small birds as well as the usual insects. A Nephila may produce 325 yards of silk thread in just one day. Luckily, for the Nephila spider, the web is so tough that it does not need to be rebuilt every day.

Weird webs

There are many extraordinary variations of spider webs. The bolas spider of Australia suspends a single sticky thread from its body to "fish" for passing insects. It even whirls the thread around when it senses a moth close by. The net-casting spider makes a rectangular web, then cuts it free from its supports. It holds one corner of this web with each of its front four legs and hangs by its back legs. It waits for insects to pass underneath and then quickly wraps them in the net and pulls them in.

Above A bolas spider dangles its sticky fishing line. It has already caught and wrapped a moth.

Right This net-casting spider has positioned its net to trap prey.

GLOSSARY

Adapted Built for a particular way of life.

Aggressive Ready to attack animals other than prey.

Antidote A substance that can stop the bad effects of a drug or poison.

Assassin A killer.

Bivouac A shelter used as a temporary home.

Camouflage A color, pattern, or shape that makes something hard to see in its surroundings.

Carnivora A group of mammals, including cats, bears, dogs, and weasels, that are adapted for meat-eating.

Carnivore A meat-eater.

Carrion A dead animal used as food.

Colony A group of ants, bees, or wasps that live and work together and function as a unit.

Constrictor A snake that suffocates its prey by squeezing it.

Digest To soften food and break it down into tiny pieces.

Engulf To surround or swallow something totally.

Evolve To develop over many generations by gradual changes.

Fang A special tooth for injecting venom (as in snakes and spiders) or for stabbing (as in cats).

Gore To pierce or stab with horns.

Grubs The larvae of insects such as beetles.

Hibernate To go into a resting state during the winter.

Hood The fold of skin on the head of a cobra.

Impala A type of small antelope found in southern and eastern Africa.

Inuit Native peoples living on the Arctic coasts of North America.

Larvae The young of animals such as insects.

Ligament A tissue made of fibers that joins two bones.

Marsupial A mammal that carries its babies in a pouch on the mother's body; for example, a kangaroo.

Nomadic Moving from place to place.

Predator An animal that catches and kills other animals for food.

Prey An animal that is caught and eaten by another animal (a predator).

Pupae Insect young that are between the larva and adult stages.

Recluse A person or animal that hides from others.

Reticulated Like a net; a reticulated python has net-like markings.

Solitary Living alone.

Spasm An uncontrollable movement of a muscle.

Spawn To lay eggs in water. It is also the name for the eggs themselves.

Spinnerets The organs spiders use to spin silk.

Suffocate To kill or be killed by lack of air.

Territory The area in which an animal lives. Some animals guard their territory.

Tranquilized Drugged so as to become calm, quiet, and sometimes sleepy.

Tubers The fleshy underground stems of some plants. Potatoes are tubers.

Venom Poison.

Vertebrate A creature with a backbone and a skeleton made of bone or cartilage.

Vitamin A The substance needed for growth in young animals and for proper function of the eyes. Too much vitamin A can be very dangerous.

FURTHER INFORMATION

BOOKS

Baker, Lucy. *Polar Bears*. New York: Puffin Books, 1990.

Bennett, Paul. *Catching a Meal*. Nature's Secrets. New York: Thomson Learning, 1994.

Gravelle, Karen and Squire, Ann. *Animal Talk*. New York: Julian Messner, 1988.

Hilker, Cathryn Hosea. *A Cheetah Named Angel*. Cincinnati Zoo Books. New York: Franklin Watts, 1992.

Losito, Linda et al. *Insects and Spiders*. Encyclopedia of the Animal World. New York: Facts on File, 1990.

McIntyre, Rick. *Grizzly Cub: Five Years in the Life of a Bear*. Seattle: Alaska Northwest, 1990.

Parker, Steve. *Cunning Carnivores*. Creepy Creatures. Milwaukee: Raintree Steck-Vaughn, 1993.

Parsons, Alexandra. *Amazing Snakes*. New York: Alfred A. Knopf Books for Young Readers, 1990.

Peissel, Michel and Allen, Missy. *Dangerous Mammals*. The Encyclopedia of Danger. New York: Chelsea House, 1993.

Perry, Philippa. *Amazing Animals*. Info Adventure. New York: Thomson Learning, 1995.

Ricciuti, Edward R. *Reptiles*. Our Living World. Woodbridge, CT: Blackbirch Press, 1993.

Stoneman, Richard. *Dangerous Animals*. Info Adventure. New York: Thomson Learning, 1995.

The Visual Dictionary of Animals. Eyewitness Visual Dictionaries. New York: Dorling Kindersley, 1991.

VIDEOTAPES

Giant Bears of Kodiak Island (National Geographic)

Lions of the African Night (National Geographic)

Growing Up Wild series (Time-Life). A 20-tape set that shows animals growing up in the wild.

CD-ROMS

Dangerous Creatures (Microsoft).

The LIFEmap Series (Time-Life). A three-CD set that shows the diversity and evolution of life.

INDEX